TRUE STORIES FROM A SOCIAL WORKER

COLIN WARD

True Stories from A Social Worker

MILTON & HUGO L.L.C.
4407 Park Ave., Suite 5
Union City, NJ 07087, USA

Website: *www. miltonandhugo.com*
Hotline: *1- 888-778-0033*
Email: *info@miltonandhugo.com*

Ordering Information:
Quantity sales. Special discounts are granted to corporations, associations, and other organizations. For more information on these discounts, please reach out to the publisher using the contact information provided above.

Library of Congress Control Number:		2024908905
ISBN-13:	979-8-89285-156-5	[Paperback Edition]
	979-8-89285-157-2	[Digital Edition]

Rev. date: 05/20/2024

To my teachers who never gave up on me even though I was not sure that this profession was what I wanted to do.

To my family who stuck by my side and helped me understand that this profession was right for me.

To my friends who, even though I may have missed several events due to my schooling or work, never faulted me for that and have been by my side all these years.

Finally, to all of those in the social-work field. You are all bad asses, and you are all heroes! Keep up the good fight and never lose that drive!

Disclaimer: The situations, cases, or experiences in this book are of the author's personal experience. Any sort of resemblance to an individual, situation, or experience is pure coincidence.

CONTENTS

INTRODUCTION

Hello! My name is Colin Ward, and I have been in the social work field for several years, and I thought I'd like to share some true experiences and stories from my time as a social worker. This story will not be laid out as normal ones. In fact, this story is going to be much, much different in the fact that I'm not going to spew information and facts at you. I'm not going to try to sway you or educate you on why social work is a great or not-so-great field. I'm not going to try and scare you either. My plan is to bring information about the social-work field to light and to bring the experience to people's awareness. I wish something like this was available when I was in school and/or before I started my path into this field.

Just a quick disclaimer, this book will have certain topics that may be hard for some readers, such as sexual abuse, drug abuse, and child/adolescent death. Please read with caution, and if needed, take some time. Your mental health is most important. You are important. Mental health matters. You matter.

PART 1

Schooling

CHAPTER

1

Hello again! I hope the disclaimer did not scare you away because I do have a lot of interesting stories to tell; however, they are not always fun, happy, go-lucky stories. We are social workers, and we see and experience things that may be hard for many to comprehend and understand. Hell, the many stories I tell, obviously with keeping true to confidentiality, to people would, nine times out of ten, always be like, "Wait, that happened? You can't be serious?!" Well guess what, Susan, it did happen. I am serious, it was real, and it happens *way* more than you think. What they don't do at the beginning of the profession is that they don't prepare you for what you are about to see (if you are doing this professionally) or what you are about to read (if you are reading this book in school).

I originally did not go to college for social work; I went for elementary education. I always had this feeling and thought that I would like to help people and I love little kids, so why not help shape their minds? Seemed like a good plan, right? I took cadet teaching in high school and worked with fifth graders and felt pretty good about my choice going into college. It was not until I started my freshman career that I quickly learned that I did *not* want to be an elementary-education teacher. Now I'm not knocking the profession. I know a lot of people who are in this field, and that is great for them! You go! However, this was not for me. I took several classes and found myself, for lack of a better word, bored out of my mind. I took a long hard look in the mirror and asked myself, "Do I really want to do this my entire life? Yeah, the summer breaks off would be nice but other than that, is it me?" After the long hard look, as well as talking to various people and various Internet searches, I stumbled into a class called "Introduction to Social Work." I never heard of this before except on movies or *Law & Order: Special Victims Unit* where you would see social workers bust in, grab a child who has been neglected, and then *bam*! Next scene, courtroom testifying. I quickly found out that this was not all that they do, as Hollywood would like to portray.

CHAPTER

2

In my "Introduction to Social Work" class, I was able to learn not only the ins and outs of the profession, but also the different sides of the profession. I also learned the history of the profession. As an individual who is a history buff, I was fascinated by in learning how old the profession is and how it can be intertwined with other professions, such as psychology and sociology. As one would expect, "Introduction to Social Work" is just a basic fundamental class that allows you to dip your toes into the water to experience what it is about. From then, you are thrown into various other subjects and subsubjects that you may not have known existed or knew existed but had no idea what they were about.

One class that I had found to be informative was called "Social Work Careers." This class, as its name states, is about various careers that you would be able to experience as a social worker. Now when I tell you that I was shocked at what all a social worker can do, I was *shocked*. I felt that social workers only did one thing, and that was child protective services. I was unaware that there was a plethora of other classes that a social worker could be, such as being an author, researcher, filmmaker, therapist, counselor, the list goes on. This class, for me at least, helped me better understand that the social work field is so vast and that if one aspect is not for you, there are other niches out there for you to fit into. Don't worry, you'll find it, and once you do, you're going to rock its socks off! That's still cool to say right? Knock your socks off? If not, it's making a comeback!

After "Careers" and my "Introduction" class, I found myself being thrown into much more rigorous and highly skilled classes, such as techniques, theories, research, statistics, and other classes that as a student, at only eighteen to nineteen, odd taking because I did not know much of the world. Hell, I'm in my thirties, and I *still* don't know much of the world. It is constantly changing, and as it changes, society changes and thus makes our jobs as social workers much harder because you have to be constantly up on the trends; but I digress. Once I was comfortable in my path in the social-work profession, rocking and rolling out classes left and right, I still had this feeling of wanting more. I felt that I had let myself down inside by not fulfilling a part of me that still wanted to be a teacher.

I, again, had a sit-down moment with myself, this time not in front of a mirror but on a long drive, and thought, *Social work? Really? What the hell would I even do? I mean I know what I could do, but is this something that I want to do until I am in my sixties or until I ultimately die?*

I drove around for several hours having this internal struggle on my life plan. I want to take a quick sidebar and say how fucked up it is that society tells us at eighteen, "Okay. You graduated high school, you're an adult now. Now figure out what the hell it is you want to do with your life!" For most of us, we don't know what we want to do. Hell, for a lot of us with careers, we still don't. But what I like about college and the world we live in now, we are able to learn more and experience things that we may not have been privy to before.

Okay, back to the main topic at hand. Sorry for the sidebars. There may be more in the book, and if so, I'm sorry. I told you this book isn't going to be like your normal read, didn't I? Anyways, where was I? Oh yeah, driving around thinking about my life choices. As I stated, I felt like I had this feeling of "What do I want to do with my life? Is this really it? Am I destined for more? Am I Batman?" Full disclosure, I am *not* Batman. He is way richer than me and way more in shape than me. I, however, kept having this thought about teaching. Now, as stated earlier, I am a history buff. I love history and everything about history, especially the twentieth century. I could sit and watch documentaries on World War I, World War II, the Vietnam War, the Cold War, and any other sort of instances from that century for days on end. I always had this feeling of being a history teacher but not for elementary school-age children, but high-school children. I felt that I had a connection with this population and that I could connect with them on a personal level.

For many, history sucks and can be found as boring. I saw that on many of my friends' faces when I was in high school and college, but then there was me sitting there with eyes the sizes of saucers absorbing all of the information that I could. In that time of me driving and self-reflecting, I thought, *Fuck it. I'll be a history teacher! Not one of those old boring, crotchety history teachers, but one of the cool, hip, laidback teachers with tattoos and would put on movies and be like, "Oh shit! You see this? Now this is what Ridley Scott had gotten right about the Gladiator culture and this is what he did not."* I wanted to connect with my students on a personal level and make my class fun. In the moment of realization, I was confident that this was my direct life plan.

I found my way into my advisor's office and switched back to teaching. I stayed in this field for only one semester. I thought that this was for me. I thought that teaching was my destiny, but I was wrong. Dead wrong. In my heart I knew that social work was for me.

The day after the end of the semester, I found myself in my academic advisor's office and talking to them about my life and sudden realization that teaching is not for me but that I think social work is. The look on my academic advisor's face was one that I will not ever forget. It was a look of "I knew you'd be back" and "I'm glad you're here." As I sat down and told them my story of how I ventured out into a new school program only to be back into my old program again was priceless. I was lucky enough to have an advisor who didn't scold me for my various decisions but was happy to find that I was back in my niche. That's what college is about anyways: finding your niche, even if it means bouncing around programs and schools.

PART 2

Internship

CHAPTER

3

As many of you know who are in social-work programs, and those who don't, you must complete an internship in your undergrad. Depending on your schooling, this must be done either at one location for one full year or it can be broken up into two different locations for the entire year. I was lucky enough to have one internship for the entire year and, boy, was that an internship! I was exposed to *a lot* of experiences, and I learned from them.

When I started my school path and research into the social-work field, I originally only knew about one career path, child protective services. It wasn't until I got to college that I was able to learn more about various career paths through my "Careers" class. I found that class to be very interesting; however, I still had this notion in my head that child protective services was the only career path for me. I felt that this was my destiny and dream. I was able to seek out an internship with a local agency and was able to spend the next year working full time, going to school as well as participating in a full year-long internship that opened my eyes to the world around me.

I started my internship path with a local child protective services agency, and I was so scared, not for the fact that I was not confident in my skills, but from what I've heard and seen in the media. I have seen these individuals as individuals who had come to snatch babies and break up families. I guess you can say that I entered this internship with a bias on what I would expect. Once I was able to enter this process, I learned more and more that this was what I felt like I wanted to do with my life.

I don't have a lot of memories about my time in the internship that I had completed; however, I do remember one thing very clearly that I didn't think I would ever think about again. One day I entered the intern site like every other day. I said hello to my friends that I made there, talked about what we were going to have for lunch, and talked about our weekend. This went on for the better part of the early mornings as it was not a court day, and we were just doing paperwork this morning. I remember my direct supervisor calling me into their office and told me to sit down. I felt like I was in the principal's office and was about to be scolded or yelled at or, even worse, let go from my internship site. As I sat there, I was thinking about all the things that it could be as my supervisor was messing around in their cabinet. After several minutes, which felt like literal hours, they brought out this *big* green binder and placed it on their desk. Now when I say *big* green binder, think of like a big legal binder, you know, the one's with the large three rings? Yeah, that size.

I asked them what this was, and they motioned me to sit in their chair. The next thing that they had said to me is something that I won't forget. They told me, "This big binder is all the fatalities that we had in our county within the past year. And I want you to look through all of these files, review them, familiarize yourself with this, and report back to me." They told me that they wanted me to "take it all in" and to "experience every aspect of the report."

I did as I was told; and for the next several hours, about four or so, I sat in their big office, alone, and reviewed hundreds upon hundreds of fatality reports. Luckily enough for me, I didn't have to see any pictures or vides of this, it was just the legal documents and written documents from the workers, but still, this was not something that I thought I would be exposed to in my very early twenties.

Once I finished the review of the hundreds upon hundreds of documents, I stepped out of the office and sat down in my designated area not sure what to think or feel. I spoke with my friend, who was a worker at the time, about what I had just had to endure, and they looked at me in my eyes and said, "Well, bud, welcome to child services. What you saw was the underbelly of the job, the real shitty things that we get to do. Now you just saw our documents and read our reports. Hell, you didn't get to see what we get to see. Next time I get a fatality, I'll take you so you can experience the real shit."

I sat there, and all I could do was just nod. I didn't know what to say. I didn't know how to act. I was just sort of not numb, but just present, if that makes sense. Now don't get me wrong, I knew child-service workers saw some messed up things. Hell, in any job you are going to be exposed to various messed-up things. But for them to be so nonchalant about the entire thing, I was sort of shocked. You must remember, I was in my early twenties, like twenty to twenty-one. I was still learning the world and all that was involved. These workers had been doing this for years and years. They were desensitized to the situations, so for them, this type of work and the experiences was just a regular Wednesday. For me, however, this was something that I would not forget.

CHAPTER

4

The rest of my time at child services had gone well for my internship. I was able to go out with various other workers, learn their strategies and styles, and see the other side of child services, not just the investigation part but the long-term side. I was also able to take on a few cases of my own. This allowed me to not only experience the profession, but also allowed me a chance to practice the skills that I had learned from them and in my schooling. I was able to do investigations on my own. Of course, I had a seasoned worker with me in the background to help, but I was doing the work. I was the one investigating. I was the one doing the long and tedious paperwork. But by gosh, I was doing it, and I was so happy. I was so happy that I found my career path. I was all set to enter their office, share a cubicle, go out with various coworkers, and have a life made.

Now you're thinking, *That's awesome, Colin! Glad to hear this! But why is there more to this book then?*

Well, little reader you, this isn't the end of my story. Oh, not by a long shot. This, my friend, is just the start.

Like I had said, I was in my zone. I was rocking and rolling my cases out, killing it at my internship, killing it in my schooling; and I felt like nothing could bring me down—until something brought me down: depression and anxiety. Now I'm not going to sit here and spew facts and statistics and numbers at you about how many individuals suffer from mental health and this number constitutes that many for depression and this many from anxiety. If you're curious, Google it. The answer may surprise you because, spoiler alert, it's a lot. Many individuals whom you interact with on a daily suffer from this and are struggling but put on a good front. This could be your brother, sister, aunt, uncle, friend, boyfriend, girlfriend, whomever. Just know that there are people out there who are struggling, so maybe instead of being a dick all the time, not saying you are a dick reader, but this is a metaphorical dick we are talking about. Does that sound weird? Metaphorical dick? I'm not sure. This may be taken out, but if not, what I'm trying to say is, be a good person. Be kind. Be compassionate. Check in on your friends whom you haven't heard from or seen in a while. Tell a stranger you love them or like their outfit, because I can guarantee you, it may just end up saving a life. I wish I learned that lesson because I lost a good friend of mine due to depression.

Back to the topic at hand however: child services and my career job/dream job. Like I said, I felt like I was killing it and was in this for the long haul; but slowly, anxiety and depression kicked in, took a room for rent, paid their tab for a long time, and never left. My time in my internship was starting to come a close, and I could feel it. I wasn't sure what I was going to do when I graduated, but I knew this wasn't for me. You're probably thinking, *Wait a minute, you have a part in your book called "Child Protection Services."* You'd be right, I do, but that time will come, right now I'm talking about my time in my internship.

CHAPTER

5

The final day at my internship was bittersweet. The day felt like any other regular day. I went into the office, sat at my little desk, grabbed a cup of coffee, and reviewed my emails. I didn't know that the last half of the day would be how it was. The first half of the day was honestly sort of boring, not a lot of commotion going on. The last half of the day, after lunch, however, was different. When I returned to the office after lunch with my two friends/mentors, I had found my desk to be covered in glitter, balloons, streamers, as well as party favors. It was like a Party City threw up on my desk, but I wasn't mad about it. In fact, I was happy to see this because it showed me that they cared about me, valued me, and liked having me around, even if my brain didn't think so.

After several laughs and talks from all of the workers in the office, I was told that I was to go to the conference room for a final assessment that needed to be completed. This was not uncommon as we sometimes had clients come to the office for interviews. I didn't think anything of this and made my way back to the conference room. When I entered, I was met with more balloons, gifts, a giant cake, and stories from my coworkers about how much they enjoyed my time with them and how much they would miss me. I won't lie, I was a little shocked and started to tear up because it was so special to see this.

The end of the day came quicker than I had thought. The fanfare had concluded. The cake was all eaten. The laughter had subsided, and the clock was getting closer to the 4:30 p.m. time. I was ready to go home. I had enough of the day; however, there was one more thing that I was not expecting to encounter. As I was about to pack my things up from my tiny desk, I was called into the main director's office and was told to sit down. At the time I was scared because I was unsure what this had meant, but then again, what could they do to me? Fire me? I wasn't even employed.

The main director's office was quiet, I can remember. It had a feeling of stillness, and one could think that this is because to the type of job that they had: supervising a profession that is heavily hated on. I was not sure what to expect, but after a few minutes of silence, the director spoke.

"We love you. Hell, I love you. You are a fantastic intern. You did so much growth through your time here. It has been such a joy to see you thrive in this environment. I don't do this, but... I want to extend you a job offer. Now I know what you're thinking, and don't worry. We don't' care that you're still in school now. You focus on that, and once you graduate, you can start back up here, no questions asked."

I was shocked. I didn't know what to think or what to say. I sort of sat there speechless. After a minute or two, you could tell that it was starting to get a little awkward with the silence in the room. Once I was able to fully process what I was told and what great opportunity I had, I made one of the biggest mistake I could have done, and that was say no. I told the director, "As much as I would *love* to have this job, I just can't at this time. My mental health is not in the best spot now, and I don't want it to get in the way of my job."

I could tell that my director was shocked. They did not know what to say, and now I could see what my director had seen just not too long ago. After a few seconds of my director and me staring at each other, they stated, "Colin...thank you. Thank you for being honest with me and with yourself. I know this career is not the best and the easiest, and to tell you the truth, it will cause you to go crazy. Hell, there's been times myself where I must sit down and reevaluate my life choices too. I don't hate you for your decision. I really don't. I want you to know that you will always have a spot here if you decide to change your mind and you are always welcome to visit."

I didn't know what to say. I never had a boss or an individual who was boss-like treat me like this before. I never had someone talk to me like this. For a moment, I thought, *Did I make the right decision by declining?* It was not until I got home and after I had time to process everything that I felt like I did the right thing, now. As you will see soon, I did return to the child protective services world but with a different county.

PART 3

Child Protection Services

Dear reader, I want to take a moment and to let you know that this section of the book, part 2, is not going to be an easy one to read, let alone write. This part will discuss my time in child protective services. Now this part will have some humorous parts, but it will also have a lot of stories and topics that may be tough for some to read. I want you to know that you are not obligated to read this section if you feel uncomfortable. If you do decide to read this section and feel uneasy or feel like it's not for you, I want you to skip ahead and forget about this one. This part will talk about various forms of abuse, such as sexual and physical abuse. This part will also talk about neglect and will touch on some stories of children who had unfortunately passed away. Please take this into consideration and take your mental health into consideration as well.

CHAPTER

6

The time at my internship site had come and gone with a flash. Once that day had finished, I found myself at graduation, then working over the summer, postgraduation. I also found myself toying with the idea entering grad school for social work. I wasn't sure that this was something that I would ever want to do, but after speaking with my professor in my undergrad, they told me that if I wanted to make *some* money, I would have to get my masters. I was reluctant at first, but after some time thinking this over, I had found myself researching various graduate courses. I found one that saw interesting and the best part was it was online! I was so happy to see that, and I immediately applied.

Once I applied, I was nervous because I was not sure what my next step would be. I wasn't sure what graduate school would be like and what my future would be. I spent the next several weeks working at my full-time job at a local grocery store just patiently waiting for a phone call or email telling me about my future.

One day while I was at work, I had received a phone call while on my break from a random number listed out of Maryland. I thought, *I don't know anyone from Maryland...who could this be?* I reluctantly answered it, thinking it was a spam caller, but I was wrong. Very wrong. It was an admissions counselor telling me that I had been accepted into their online graduate Master of Social Work program. I was ecstatic. I was so shocked and happy I spend the rest of my day at work on cloud nine.

CHAPTER 7

The rest of the weeks after my phone call had felt like it had flown by. I was getting myself ready for my new chapter in my life and that was as a graduate student. I was scared as anyone would be but still super excited. I was furthering my career, what else could I be happier about? Well, I guess if I won the lottery, that would have been pretty awesome, and I would have been super happy, but sadly, I've never won.

My online program started in August, and like any other start to a school program, it was a lot of intro classes and classes to ease you into the program as well as their schooling. I didn't mind this as much as I already had a degree in social work. I felt like I knew so much. I felt like this program was going to be a breeze.

I found myself flying through the program until I found myself in California for a weeklong conference where I was able to show off my social-work skills. I didn't really know anybody, so I kept to myself a lot after the conferences. I found myself watching a lot of television and movies. I also found myself looking at various jobs that I could have with a bachelor's in social work because I knew I didn't want to continue working at my local grocery store forever. I found myself on Google and found my way to my state's website and found the page for jobs. I scrolled through a bunch of various jobs until I came across one for child protective services. I thought in that moment, *I can totally do this! I just completed a yearlong internship, I'd be perfect for this job!* So I applied.

I applied to this job, closed my laptop, and went to bed, not thinking anything of it. I woke up the next morning and continued my time in my conference. I didn't think much of the job application as this was the first application I've ever completed for a "big job" like this. It was a job with the state after all. I was just focused on my conference.

The conference came to an end, and I found myself on a flight back home. I boarded the flight and made my way back home. I was so tired from all the traveling when I had returned home I went to bed and fell asleep. Hard. When I woke up several hours later, I saw that I had a missed call from child protective services. I was expecting them to call me thanking me for my job application however they had gone on a different route. That was not the case. They had left me a voicemail stating that they loved my application and wanted to interview me—today. I listened more to the voicemail, and they said that they would like me in the office by 3:00 p.m. for an interview. I looked at the clock, and it was 2:30 p.m.

I freaked out! I ran to my closet and changed into a suit. I grabbed what resumes I had and sped, very fast, to the office for the interview. I made it to the office just in time, gained composure, and interviewed.

The interview went well, and I was offered a job on the spot in the assessment side. These were the ones we were sent out to investigate, and if there was any truth or cause to the report, we would act. I thankfully accepted the position and was told of my start date. I was so happy.

CHAPTER

8

My start date had finally come, and I was ready. I felt prepared for this. This was my moment. I found that with starting in child protective services, you had to spend three months in training, back and forth from my state's capital and the county that I was employed. The training was interesting in the state capital as it was done in a classroom setting. They provided us with information and things to look out for while investigating, but they didn't really prepare us for what it would be like. Like did you know that if you go to a home and it smells like cat pee but there aren't any cats to be found, there's a chance that they are making meth in the home? That's one cool fact I learned.

My training came to an end with various shadowing opportunities in my county. I felt moderately okay with being on my own but knew that I had quickly get it together as I would be on my own very soon. I did deep breathing and told myself, "You got this! You know what you're doing. Don't doubt yourself." I felt better, and before I knew it, my first assessment came. It was a physical abuse case where a child had broken its leg, but it was a spiral fracture, which for those not in the medical field, this happens when a bone is broken in a twisting fashion. As you can imagine, the individual involved was found guilty, and repercussions happened.

In my time, I was able to investigate several other physical abuse cases. Many of them were unfounded as there were not a lot of marks left on the child. One personal side note here. For physical abuse to be considered true, there has to be marks left on the child. If there are no marks, there is nothing to go off of. Is that bullshit? In some instances, yes. Is it right? Personally, no, but that's how it is.

The next type of reports that I would get was that of neglect. Now neglect can be anything from leaving children at home alone, there being no food or water in the home, a child being locked in closet under the stairs like Harry Potter or, my favorite, dirty homes. You're probably thinking to yourself, *Dirty homes? You like dirty homes? Are you crazy?* To answer your question, yes. Yes, I am. It is like a seek and find. You never know what you will find. Will it be toys in the fish tank? Or will it be dog poop on the walls? Guess what? It's both. I've seen both, and I loved every minute of it. The sights, the smells, the environment. It was *awesome*! Now, yes, I'm weird, I get that; and that may not be your thing, but this is the truth of the matter. You will see some crazy, messed-up stuff, and I'm here to give you a little look into what you may see.

CHAPTER 9

One story that I remember vividly was that of a dirty home. Now when I say dirty, I mean *dirty*. This home was extremely dirty. This home should have been condemned for how bad it was. And the smell, oh, don't get me started on the smell. I wish I could explain to you how it is, but I can't because, one, it's been several years and, two, it was such a distinct smell I can't even begin to describe.

My coworkers and I entered the home with the police and were immediately met with an ungodly smell. I remember one of the police officers had to step out of the home and throw up because of the smell. I however was in my prime. I was so happy to be there. I remember taking it all in. The living room was filthy. It had stained furniture, dog feces all over the floor, a fish tank had what looked like a human turd floating, and there was not a place to sit. There was just only a small path where one could walk. The basement was not better. The home was a bi-level so when you entered the home, you could go downstairs or upstairs to the main living area. The stairs toward the basement had dog feces on each step, as if their dog had decided to poop on each step to let you know, "This is my step. I have many like it, but this is mine."

My coworkers and I made our way to the basement trying to step around and not on the dog feces and trash that was strewn all over the floor. A part of our job was to take pictures of the environment as well; and so we would take a few steps, take a few pictures, and try to navigate our way around the home. We made it to the back room, which we thought was a bathroom but wasn't sure as we just saw a toilet in the room. It was very bizarre, but what was more bizarre was that the toilet appeared to have been overflowed with human feces, and it had stained the toilet. A toilet that was once pristine white and was now stained a brown color. I asked my coworker if they saw pieces of corn, and they just looked at me and said, "Let's go up to the kitchen."

I wish we hadn't because the kitchen looked like an episode out of *Hoarders*. The kitchen had about four inches of trash all over the floor; and the kitchen sink was full of dirty dishes, which were piled not only in the sink but also on the floor, the counter, and anywhere else you could think of. The dishes had live maggots covered in them along with food stuck to them. We took pictures of this and made our way to the refrigerator, which was, if you could believe it, much worse. The refrigerator was unplugged and overstuffed with food. The entire refrigerator was full of moldy food, and I swear we saw cockroaches crawl out from underneath a bag of food of who knows what. We didn't want to guess.

As we made our way through the house, taking pictures of the nastiness that we could see, we made our way to the bedrooms. The bedrooms did not have any doors to their rooms. They just had pieces of plywood across the entryway as their doors. The home was home to three children, ages ranged from fifteen to four. Each bedroom was worse than the others. They were covered in food, trash, dirty clothes, and toys. One of the bedrooms, the fifteen-year-old, didn't have a complete bed set, just a mattress. Now you're probably thinking, *Collin, what's wrong with that? Lots of people just have a mattress on their floor.* You'd be correct, reader, lots of people would have that. However, this individual just had a mattress onto of what appeared to be three feet of trash and toys. The child was literally sleeping on filth.

As we concluded our investigation, it was a no brainer that the child and her siblings had to be removed from their parents' home for their safety. It was an easy choice for us to complete as we had a duty to the children, but for the children, this was a tough thing to endure. One thing that stuck with me after all these years was what the child had said to me when I went back with them to gather clothes and a personal item or two. The child had stopped halfway gathering clothes and started to cry. I let them cry as this was a very difficult thing to endure for them. The child looked at me and said, "I'm sorry. I'm sorry for all of this, and

I'm sorry that we are dirty people. This is how we live. We are happy. We didn't know better. We are happy. We are happy with our parents. We just didn't know. We didn't know."

That hurt. That comment was something that I was unprepared for. The child and her siblings and their parents knew that they were living in filth and squalor; however, to them, this was home. This was what they were used to. They didn't know any better, and to uproot them from their home to bring them to a "normal" foster home was devastating.

The court hearing for this family was rough for all of those involved. The hearing involved not only my testimony but also the testimony from the police officers, the parents, and the fifteen-year-old. Usually, children are not involved in the hearings, but they had insisted, and the judge had granted this. This hearing was tough to listen to, and the pictures that my coworker and I had taken were passed around as well. It brought everyone back to the environment, and in that moment, I found myself smelling the smells from the home again. I didn't care to follow the case past the initial court hearing—not because I didn't care, I did. I just had other reports that I had to focus on.

This next chapter is going to be a tough one to write about and for some to read. It will talk about sex abuse of children. If you need to skip this, please do.

CHAPTER 10

As a child protective services worker, you will be exposed to various cases, environments, sights, smells, and individuals. One thing that you will be exposed to and that is inevitable is that of sexual abuse. Now you're probably thinking, *Sex abuse? I've heard about this before, but this doesn't happen in my community or my town*. Guess what? You're wrong. It does happen, and it does happen a lot more than you think. You just don't know about it.

One sex abuse story that I would like to share with you follows a seven-year-old girl, her parents, and the parents' girlfriend. Now this story did not involve me directly as I was not the one who been a part of the investigation, I was just a byproduct of the investigation. I was there as support.

One day I was going to lunch and saw one of my coworkers come in the office with a little girl. The coworker appeared to have a frazzled look on her face and had asked me, "You going to lunch?" I replied with a nod, and she returned the nod by saying, "Okay, good. Can you do me a favor and get her some lunch, please?" I agreed and asked her what she would like. She said a McDonald's Happy Meal. I was more than happy to get her a meal. My coworker thanked me and told me that she would fill me in later. A part of me felt like I wanted to know what she meant by this and a part of me did not. I wish I did not find out about her story as it was one that has never left my mind after all these years.

When I returned from McDonalds with two Happy Meals in tow, I found the little girl in the playroom that we had in the office, and I asked her if she would like to watch a movie while we ate our lunch. She agreed, and we put on *Mulan*. The little girl and I sat in the playroom, eating our McDonalds, and watching *Mulan* like there was not a care in the world. Did I have work to complete and work on? Yes, but this was more important. Being there for a child who had endured something horrible (at the time I did not know what it was) was more important.

Once the movie ended, she looked at me and said, "Now what?" I looked around the playroom and asked her if she would like to play with Barbies, dolls, or color. The little girl looked at me like I was crazy and said, "Uhm, all three, duh!" I laughed and said, "Okay, we can do all three." We spent the next several hours playing with Barbies, playing house, coloring, and playing with other dolls and toys that the office had to our disposal. After several hours of playing, the coworker who had brought her to me told me that it was time to go as she was able to get ahold of a foster family and she had to take her to them. The little girl came up to me, gave me a hug, and thanked me for the lunch and the fun time with the movie, Barbies, and playtime. I thanked her back and told her thank you for such a fun day.

The next day at the office was just like any other day. It was one with paperwork and meetings. After our morning meeting, the coworker from yesterday pulled me aside and thanked me for yesterday. She told me that the child could not stop talking about how much fun they had yesterday with me and that this really made her day. I was so happy to hear this. But this feeling quickly turned as the coworker told me the child's story.

The coworker sat me down and told me that the child from yesterday was severely sexually abused by her mother, father, and their girlfriend. The child would be locked up in a dog kennel and left in a room for hours on end with nothing to eat or drink while her parents and their girlfriend would go out to the bars. The coworker went on to tell me that her parents and their girlfriend would have sex with each other in front of the child and make her watch. They would even sometimes include the child in the session so it would be three adults and the little girl.

The child's father would constantly rape his own daughter and would make a mold of his own penis and would use it on his own daughter. The child's father would also make the child perform oral sex on him for her to get "time" out of the dog kennel. The child's mother and the parents' girlfriend would sexually abuse her by performing oral sex on her own daughter and making her perform oral sex on her and their partner. The parents would also allow friends of theirs to come into their home and "have their way" with their daughter as they thought this would help her transition into womanhood. The family would also film the acts with their daughter and would watch them together and would masturbate to the footage, all while their daughter was locked in a kennel, in a separate room, like an abused animal. The coworker told me that in her fifteen plus years in this profession, she had seen some "fucked-up shit" but this by far was the most "fucked up."

I sat there shocked. I didn't know what to say or what to think. The little girl from yesterday, the one who had a great time playing with Barbies, dolls, coloring, and watching Disney movies was severely sexually abused. The child did not appear to have suffered any sort of trauma or fear anyone. She appeared to be a normal little girl with normal little girl hopes, dreams, and aspirations. I told my coworker that there must've been some mistake. This could not have been the same little girl. She assured me that this was and that this abuse had started when she was four years old, so she had been so used to it, she didn't know any better. For her, this was "normal," and she didn't realize how wrong this was. I remember sitting there after my coworker left and just thought, *Wow, people are fucked up. How can a person do that to their own child and think it was okay? Like what?* I didn't ask my coworker how the case progressed. I didn't want to know. All I wanted to know was that the little girl was now safe from harm and safe from sick people like her family. I was assured that she was.

CHAPTER

11

The next few stories are going to be somewhat all over the place, so I'm sorry if it's not clear and concise as other stories you have read. These are stories that, as I was writing this, remembered and thought, *They would be good additions to really show you what you may see as a social worker if you decide to do the child protective services path.*

Meth

As we know, drugs are not good for you or your health, especially meth. Meth is one of the worst drugs out there, one that can have lasting effects on not only those who use it, but also their families. Now I touched on meth a little earlier and mentioned that if you enter a house and smell cat pee but don't see a cat, there is a chance that they are making meth. Well, this is a story of how I entered a meth house but was not aware of it because I saw cats around the home.

I had received a call at 2:15 a.m. in regards to a family allegedly making meth out of their home, and they had a young child in the home as well. With this nature of the report, I had only one hour to make contact with the alleged perpetrator. I woke up out of a deep sleep, put on clothes, and made my way in the middle of the night, during a snowstorm, to the home. Now with the nature of the report, you are to ensure that police come to the home with you in case this happened to be true and you needed to be escorted safely.

I entered the subdivision of where the house was around 3:00 a.m. and waited for the police officer. The snowstorm was coming down harder now, and all I could think about was when the officer would arrive. Thankfully, the police officer arrived shortly after and escorted me to the house. We knocked on the door and was surprised to be met with the father of the young child. I had told him my name, who I was with, and the nature of the report. They allowed the officer and me into the home, and we did an investigation. I had to interview both parents, and with the child being so young, I was unable to talk to them, but I was able to take pictures of the home for my records. The home appeared to be normal, and I didn't have a "gut feeling" of the home being a meth house.

I finished my investigation and played with the cat that they had in the home. I thanked them for their time and apologized for the early-morning wake-up, but we had to complete the report. They were more than understanding. The officer and I made our way back to our vehicles, and we were talking about various cases we have been in and the stuff we've seen. I'm not sure what made me turn back to the home, but I turned back to the home and noticed that the house that we had just come from had a dry patch on their roof. I'm not sure how I didn't see this initially, but this was very odd to see, especially in a snowstorm. I told the police officer about this, and he had the same thought that I did. We missed something. Now for those who don't know, if you see a house in the middle of a snowstorm with a "dry patch" on their roof and it was not covered in snow, there is a chance that they are making meth or other drugs.

The police officer and I made our way back to the house, this time with more caution because we were not sure if this was a meth house or not. We knocked on the door and were met with the same individual from before. We told the individual that we apologize but we forgot something in the home and we needed to go back and get it. The individual understood and let us back into the home. Now I want to take a moment and say, if you are suspecting that a house is an alleged meth house, *do not go back into the home. Get far away from it as possible and call 911 immediately! Do not do what I did!* You are probably thinking, *Well, yeah, this could explode any minute.* And you're right, meth houses are very scary and can explode at any minute, but you see, we didn't know that this was a meth house—until we did.

The police officer and I were more on edge now than before, and we took every corner and room with caution. We made sure to check and double-check every inch of that upstairs several times, but when we made our way to the basement, that's when things became scary. As we approached the door, the individual who opened the door for us initially started to become more and more nervous and started to become hostile. As I approached the door, the individual grabbed a knife and stood in front of the door. The police officer told him to move, or he'd get tased. The individual started to become more hostile and lunged at me. In an instant, the police officer shot his Taser at the individual, and he dropped like a sack of potatoes. As the individual was on the ground convulsing, I stepped over him and opened the basement door to see an active meth lab. I closed the door, notified the police officer, bent down, laid my business card on the individual's chest, and said, "I'll see you in court."

Back-up came quickly for the police officer and helped me take the child to my car. I thought my night was over once I got back to the office and found a placement for the child, which wasn't hard to do as many individuals love babies. I was told that before I did that, I would have to get decontaminated due to being exposed to an active meth lab. I didn't know what that meant, but I found myself being decontaminated before going back to my business. Don't worry, I'm fine and the child was fine as well. The child was sent to a nice foster family, and the child's family was taken to jail for drugs. The home, however, I'm not sure about. I haven't been past that area since.

Death of a Child

The next two stories are not easy ones to talk about as they talk about the dark side of child protective services, and that is fatalities. If you don't know what that means, in simpler terms it means having to investigate the death of a child. One story that I will talk about I was actively involved in and the other was one that I was exposed to. The latter one is not as in detail as the first, but it still is sad and it's a heavy topic.

As a worker in the child services protective agency field, we are exposed to certain cases that stick with us forever, and unfortunately, this is one of them. It involves the death of a three-year-old boy, who was the sweetest and cutest kid, and the aftermath of his passing. As I mentioned earlier in this book, I'm not trying to scare you or turn you off from this profession. It is a great profession, I just want you to be prepared for instances that you may occur, such as fatalities.

One day at the office, I had received a report of a fatality. Now, fatalities are the worst sorts of reports because there is so much involved in the case that it encompasses you. I had received a report of a three-year-old boy who had a medical condition and was brought to the hospital DOA (dead on arrival). The emergency department had done all they could do, but unfortunately, they could not do anything more. By procedure, they had to contact child protective services, and we had to investigate in case there was some foul play. Now I want to take a moment and say how horrible it is for an individual to go to a grieving mother who just lost their child to a medical condition and essentially be like, "I know this is hard, but we are going to investigate if you killed or had a part in the death of your young child." I'm sorry, but that is utter and complete shit. I get that if the parent had a part in this, but this situation was different, the child had a documented condition, yet I still had to do my investigation.

I had treated the investigation like I would with any other investigation, but one part that is different is that of the autopsy. One aspect in investigating a fatality is that you must obtain a copy of the autopsy records. You're thinking, *What?* I thought at that moment too. "Oh, you mean just paperwork form the coroner talking about the autopsy?" No. You get the full autopsy, pictures, and videos. I was unaware of this as this was my first fatality. So I was in my office eating lunch with my friend/coworker and received a copy of the report. I usually worked through lunch, so I put the CD in my computer and figured my coworker and I would read the report as we ate our lunch. Some lunchtime reading if you will. The CD was quite the opposite. It recorded the full autopsy of a three-year-old boy.

The CD was not just a series of records like I thought; but it had several pictures of the autopsy and, at the end, a video of the autopsy.

I saw this naked child lying on a cold metallic table, and as I clicked through the slides, I could see the child's skin be removed from his skull. I saw his skull cut open and his brain taken out. I saw his chest opened in the *V* shape that they do and saw all of his internal organs taken out. I saw them being held by the coroner's hands, and I saw them lying them on the scale that was next to the body. As much as I wanted to stop looking and to look away, I couldn't. I had to finish the CD. It was a part of my job. I needed to finish.

I finished the CD with reservation and just sat at my desk thinking, *What did I watch? What did I watch?* Now I have seen some messed-up things in my life. I enjoy a good horror movie or a movie with instances of gore. I've also seen crime-scene pictures and videos; but that was all on the Internet and, to my knowledge, fake. This was real. This was a real child in the community that I was living in. This was the dark side of child protective services. I finished the report and knew that this job was not for me. I could not sit back and see more dead children, let alone babies. I knew that this was going to break me and affect my mental health. At that moment, I started looking for a new job.

The final story that I'd like to mention in this part is that of another fatality that involved a child who was trying to protect his sister from an oncoming train. As stated earlier, this case was not one that I was a part of. I was just told of it, and I was able to see the crime-scene photos of the aftermath. The backstory of this was that two young children, I believe no older than five, left their home and started to play on the train tracks from behind their home. The children were playing on the train tracks when a train started to appear in the distance. The children, not knowing what to do, froze. The older child of the two pushed the other out of the way and then covered their ears out of fear. The older child unfortunately was struck by the train and sadly passed away. The younger child had survived, thanks to the older child.

The worker who had the report had the photos on their desk and would often show others as we would talk about the cases that we were working on. We seemed like one big happy family. I was able to view the photos, and to my surprise, they weren't graphic or anything of that nature. The child who had been struck by the train appeared to be sleeping next to the railroad tracks and appeared to have a few bruises on their body. I was expecting more trauma to the body, but that was not the case. The only thing that was prevalent was on the train's cowcatcher, which had an imprint of the child's face on it. There was no blood or anything like this, just an imprint.

This was another case that stuck with me and a case that I will never get out of my head. I knew from my previous fatality and other cases that this profession was not for me, even though I thought it was. During my time in child protective services, I was working full-time with them and going to school full-time. Thankfully, the end of my graduate degree came quicker than I had thought, and once I had finished, I had obtained my Master of Social Work (MSW) degree. I knew that child protective services was not for me and that I wanted to work in the medical field. I had applied to various hospitals, and much to my surprise, I was offered a job at a local hospital. I had accepted the position before even knowing the salary. I just knew that I was finally out of that career and onto another one.

PART 4

Hospitals

CHAPTER 12

The last few days of my times at child protective services was okay. I wasn't given more cases as there was no need. I finished my cases that I could, and the ones that I was unable to finish, I handed them off to my colleagues. They may have been mad at me for this; however, they stayed, and I didn't. I was able to get out and keep my mental health somewhat intact.

I started my new position at a local hospital as a social-work case manager, and if you were interested in getting into this line of work once you receive your master's degree, do it. It is an awesome and rewarding profession. It can be heartbreaking at parts, but being able to see people and interact with them was one of the best parts. One of the worst parts however was the fact that you had to go into a hospital every day for work. For many this can be tough and hard to deal with seeing as how you are exposed to sick and sometimes dying people all day, but if you can get past that, you will do fine.

I had labeled this part of the book "Hospitals," as in plural. I was able to work for two local hospitals. The first one I was strictly doing social work-related activities such as placing people in nursing homes, working on getting them into hospice, stuff like that. Sometimes you would have an adoption here and there, but that was rare. The other hospital I worked at was like the first but also included more nursing roles. I was tasked with ordering home health-care services, IV antibiotics, oxygen machines, as well as my regular duties, such as arranging home health, hospice services, and nursing facilities. This part of the book I will provide several stories from both hospitals. Some of these stories will be funny, and some will be sad, but I wanted to give you a look into what you may encounter if you enter this side of social work.

CHAPTER

13

As many hospitals across the country go, you have different floors or units for specific issues. You may have a medical/surgical floor, a pediatrics floor, an oncology floor, and an ICU floor. The first hospital that I had worked at was like any other hospital. They had several floors, and each floor had a separate designated unit. The unit that I was assigned to was the oncology unit. This unit was one where I would interact with mostly older individuals who were suffering from different forms of cancer. We also housed individuals who had stomach and GI issues, so we had a lot of individuals who had a colonoscopy.

One story that I would like to share from my time at this first hospital is in regard to an individual who had cancer. This individual was an older lady. I'd say in her late nineties, who was the most spry and happy-go-lucky person you would ever met. She was from Britain, and she had a thick accent that you could only smile at because she was the cutest old lady. I would go in and do my rounds, and she would flirt every day while the *Price Is Right* played in the background. One day, however, after my rounds, I decided to stop in and talk to her because she was just one of those old ladies that you *had* to talk to and learn about their past.

When I entered the room, I saw her sitting up in her bed with her hair in curlers watching some random trash TV. She said to me in her old British accent, "You Americans have nothing on TV to watch…just trash television." I laughed and agreed. I sat down next to her and asked her if I could hear some stories of her and her life, if she would like to tell any. One story that I remember vividly was one that you only hear about in the movies, books, or television.

I took my seat across from her, and she asked me to hold her hand. I complied because when an elderly lady asks to hold your hand, you hold that hand. It's like when a child hands you a toy telephone, you take that phone call and act like you're talking to a high-level executive about the new sale that just happened. *Buy! Buy! No! Yes! Now sell!* It's just something that you do. Okay, back to the story.

I saw down next to her, and she told me a story of her brother and her life when she was a little girl. I want to let you know that this story is coming from memory and the story is not mine, just what I remember. The elderly lady told me that she grew up in England during the time of World War II. She had stated that she remembered one day, when she was a little girl, she and her brother were playing in their garden in England and they heard the raid sirens. When she and her brother tried to get back to their bunker or basement, it was too late. The Blitzkrieg was upon her. She stated that she remembered seeing the planes fly over her city and the bombs dropping in waves.

The elderly lady went on to state that she knew that she had no time to take her and her brother to safety, so instead, they hid the best they could with some sort of cover in the garden. The next thing that she could remember was that she woke up covered in rubble, her brother's limp body next to her, and her home left in rubble as well. Apparently, one of the bombs from the Blitzkrieg had been dropped next to her garden or in her garden and had gone off. The now elderly lady stated that she had looked around and just saw destruction for as far as she could see. She had lost her brother, her home, and more than likely her parents. She was unsure if they had survived or not because she never saw them again.

As I sat there, I could see one tear fall down her cheek. You could tell that she has told this story to her friends, family, and anyone who would listen several times before. This story for her was nothing new; it was part of her life, but you could tell that she was still affected of the aftermath. She was affected by losing her home, brother, family, and all her belongings. This was impactful, not only for her, but for anyone who would hear her story because this was something that happened to a real person—a real person whom I was able to interact with, hold hands with, be a friend in her last moments.

I came back in the next day to see my friend, but I noticed that the room had a new person in it. I spoke with the nurse on the floor about her, and they told me that she had passed away last night in her sleep. I was assured that she was not in any sort of pain or discomfort, but she was at peace. Maybe she needed to have her story be told one final time before she passed on. Maybe she just needed company in her last night, and she knew it was her time. No one knows, but what I do know is that I will never forget her and how much light she brought into this world.

CHAPTER

14

I wish that I could say that I didn't have more stories like the one I had just mentioned, but unfortunately, that's not the case. As a social worker, we get sad stories like this all the time. We get to experience very negative things such as death and sickness, but we have to stay strong. We must remain tough, and as much as it kills us, do what we can for our patients. This is true for working on an oncology unit. You will work with difficult clients, and you will work with clients who are nasty, but you also have to remember, their loved ones are actively going through chemotherapy or they were just told that they had like a few months to live.

You will be exposed to instances like this on a daily if you enter this field. I have thousands more stories of hospice talk and talking to family members of their loved ones that were just given terrible news, but I thankfully, I have blocked them out, or they have become so second nature to me that I don't think about them. I do however have a few funny stories and a few gross stories about working in hospitals, and they are all in the net chapter. Let's start with gross and then end on funny because I want to end on a happy note.

CHAPTER 15

Like I said, I have plenty of funny and gross stories, but I will talk about some gross stories. I'm not going to designate which hospital these next several stories come from because to be honest with you, I don't remember. All I can remember is the stories of what I was able to see and smell, and let me tell you, the smells sometimes were worse than the seeing.

One story that I remember vividly was that of a patient who I called Popcorn Man. I don't want you to think that we give nicknames to patients when they enter the hospital, but this man, he deserved the name of Popcorn Man and rightfully so. The story takes place in the intensive care unit (ICU), and I was tasked with doing an initial assessment, where you ask the clients background information of their lives.

I thought this would be an easy interaction, because sometimes we would get actually nice people and not total assholes who hated being in the hospital. This man was the former. He was super sweet, nice, and funny. Except there was one thing that stood out, and that was his legs. A little background information on this individual. He was about four hundred pounds, and his legs were so large he had no ankles. It was sad to see, but unfortunately, sometimes we get patients like this, and we have to treat them. What had thrown me off when I entered the room was not his size—I've seen many large people in my time working in the hospital—but it was a distinct smell, a smell of buttery popcorn.

I looked around the room and did not see any popcorn buckets, kernels, or any instance of popcorn in the room. I stepped out and asked the nurse if they smelt any buttery popcorn in his room. The nurse laughed and just said, "Pull back his blanket by his legs." I didn't think anything of it and pulled back the blanket—with the individual's permission, of course—and what I saw was something that I didn't think I'd ever see. It looked like scales all over this man's legs, but they were flakey and smelt like buttery popcorn. I asked the nurse what this could be, and she said, "Oh, sweetie, he has cellulitis. This is very common." I asked if the smell was, and she told me no, but that he had some fungal infection as well. I simply said, "Oh, okay…cool, cool…," and went on with my assessment. The interaction with this man and his legs had turned me off from movie-theater-style butter popcorn for years. It was truly disgusting. Hope you don't think of this man and his legs the next time you go to your local movie theater.

One other gross story involves bedsores. If you don't know what bedsores are, they are pressure injuries that happen when you don't get enough blood flow to certain parts of your bodies. This is commonly seen with bedridden patients, and that is why you hear nurses and aids saying that they have to turn the patient. They don't want them to get bed sores. This next story involves bedsores that had gotten so bad, you could stick your head in it like a lion show at the circus.

One patient that I had the pleasure of interacting with was a younger female. I would say about midfiftes, who had been paralyzed from the neck down after an accident. This young female had spent about half of her life in a nursing home due to the immense care that she needed. I have had this individual before plenty of times, and so I had a rapport with her. I would try to make her laugh and smile and sometimes was successful. I remember one day I went in to talk with her, and wound care was in the room. I asked if I should come back and both the patient and the wound care nurse said no. Sidebar, if a patient is being worked on with wound care, don't go in. You don't want to see what they are doing because it can be gnarly.

I entered the room, due to lack of better judgment, and saw something that I wish I didn't. What I had seen was this young patient's bedsores, but they weren't like normal bedsores; they were tunnels. I could see through her back. The wound care nurse told me that this was one of the nastiest things that they had ever seen and asked me if I wanted to see something "cool yet gross." Now me being me and curious, I said, "Sure! Why not?" I wish I didn't. The wound care nurse (thankfully, she was wearing a full-body gown) had taken her arm and put it through this young lady's back. She said, "The bedsores are so bad, I can stick my entire arm up until my elbow through her back! See?" She waved like it was some magic trick. I left that room and never went back into a room when I saw the wound-care nurse's cart outside the door. I always came back later.

CHAPTER

16

Okay, I know what you're thinking, *Why are you telling us about this gross stuff and when can we get the funny stories?* I'm telling you this gross stuff so you don't be shocked at what you could potentially see. And the funny stories? Well, funny to me, are up next. So, buckle up, grab some popcorn (hopefully not buttery popcorn), and let's go.

One funny story that I remember distinctly is in regards to balls, and when I say balls, I mean testicles. This story may not be funny for some people, but you have to remember, I worked in a hospital. I saw some crazy stuff, sometimes funny and sometimes not. This one, however, to me was one of the funniest things I encountered.

One day as I was doing my rounds in the hospital, I met an elderly gentleman who was set to go home, and in doing so, he needed certain home health services and equipment at home, such as a shower bench, cane, and raised toilet seat so he could get up and off the toilet easier. I entered the room and spoke with the individual and told him that he was set to go home later on today and if there was any sort of equipment that he would like. What came out of his mouth next made me laugh so hard I had a hard time trying to contain myself.

The elderly man simply stated, "Well, son…I tell ya what. My balls. That's right, my balls. You see, I'm eighty years old, and my boys—as you young kids call them—aren't like how they used to be. They don't sit all nice and pretty. Oh no, they sag, and they sag far! You see, when I sit to use the bathroom, my balls, they float. They float in the toilet bowl, and when I urinate, I urinate on my balls. I really don't want to urinate on my balls anymore, son. They don't need to get dunked in the water, let alone pissed on."

I tried to keep my composure and not laugh, but let me tell you, when an eighty-year-old man is talking to you about his testicles sagging too much in that they float in the toilet bowl, you can't help but laugh.

I tell the individual, "Don't worry sir, I will do all that I can do ensure that we can protect your balls from harm."

The old man thanked me, and I went to see what I could do to help him.

After several minutes of trying to find a raised toilet seat, I brought one back to him and told him of the good news.

The elderly man looked up at me from his newspaper and just said, "Son, I thank you. Not only do I thank you, but my balls thank you. I no longer have to sit on the toilet and have my balls get dunked in the cold toilet water and then have them be pissed on. From the bottom of my heart, I thank you, and my balls especially thank you."

I left the room laughing all the way back to my office at the conversation that I just had. You see, sometimes you will have good days, funny days in the social-work field in the hospital realm but also you got bad days and gross days. I hope this little insight helped you see what you may experience out in the wild. And if an elderly man thanks you for helping him and his balls, you just say you're welcome and leave.

PART 5

Nursing Homes

CHAPTER

17

As stated earlier, I worked for two different hospitals but felt like I needed to do more. I wanted to continue to help people, and I've sent a lot of people to nursing homes for care. I wanted to experience this side of the profession, and so I left my job as a social worker at my hospitals and entered a new realm of social work: nursing-home social work. I was lucky to stay with one nursing home for a little over a year and then left to go to another one where I only lasted about four hours due to the conditions of that nursing home. I'll get into that shortly.

I had the privilege of working in a nursing home, one where I was the director of social services and where I stayed for over a year, and the other one where I was hired into as a social services director but left on my first day because of the horrendous environment that this facility had. The first facility wasn't the best, but it certainly was not the worst. That was the second facility.

Now I have plenty of stories from my time in the nursing homes, but I would like to talk about three: one somewhat funny (again, funny to me), one really sad, and then the final one being as to why I only lasted only four hours.

CHAPTER 18

The first nursing home that I had the privilege to work for was very local. So local in the sense that I was able to make it to work in about five minutes from where I was living. This was nice because I could sleep in and still make it to work on time. This nursing home, like many other nursing homes, have a wide cast of characters that you could interact with. Think of *One Flew over the Cuckoo's Nest* but not in a mental institution. That is what working at the nursing home and interacting with the residents was like. One resident in particular that I'd like to talk about briefly is that of a seventy-five-year-old gay man whom we shall call Phil.

You will notice that this is the first time I've mentioned an individual by a name, and there is a reason for this. Phil was quite the resident. Phil had resided at the nursing home for the past fifteen years and was set on the long-term residential side. Phil had a very strange obsession with dolls and was an openly proud gay man. I want to take a minute to say that I support the LGBTQI+ community, and I do not want you to think that I am not an ally/supporter. The only reason that I mention Phil's sexuality is because it is important to this story.

At this facility, I had my own office where certain residents would come in to either talk or bring me treats or to ask about their case. Several times the residents were to come in to talk because they were bored. They don't have family or friends who would visit often, and we were their family. Phil was one of those individuals who would come to my office almost daily to just talk and ask questions. When I was working at this facility, I was one of the youngest people there by probably twenty or so years. Whenever there was a technology issue, I was the one who handled it, and Phil always had technology issues.

Phil would stop in my office several times a day because his cell phone would not work or it would be too slow and would need help with clearing his data. I would stop what I would be doing and help him out. I felt as the resident young person, it was the least that I could do. Well, one day, I got more than I bargained for.

Phil came into my office and said, "Collin! My phone! My damn phone is slow again! I need help! I can't get my videos to work!"

I calmly asked him to see his phone and if I could be of any assistance. Phil gladly handed his phone over and let me work on fixing his phone and getting his video to work. As I was going through his pictures to help clear up his data—with his permission, mind you—I was met with what seemed like hundreds upon hundreds of gay porn pictures, shirtless men with rock hard abs, several erect penises, and pictures of gay oral sex.

I asked Phil if he would be okay if I were to delete any of these pictures, and Phil looked at me like I was crazy.

He told me, "Delete? You want to delete my only nice thing about this place? No!"

I left his pictures alone, per his wishes. I then made my way to his video not working and was met with his Internet tab on his phone open with about nine Pornhub videos trying to play at once.

I asked Phil if he really needed all these videos, and he again looked at me like I was crazy.

He said, "My videos? My beautiful, beautiful videos? I guess I can get rid of a few."

I helped him clear these up and then dwindled from nine videos to only one.

I helped him get this video back working, and he thanked me before he went back to his room. On his way back to his room, Phil stopped, looked at me, showed me his phone, and said, "You know, you are very pretty for a young man. You could do videos like this as well. You care to watch with an old man like me?"

I politely declined and said, "No, thank you, Phil, I got work to do."

He nodded and walked back to his room. Ever since this one interaction, Phil would come with his phone full of pornography and would ask for help, and of course, he would get the help.

CHAPTER

19

That story was somewhat a funny one in the fact that Phil was so upfront and didn't give two cares what you thought. He was an openly gay elderly man who loved looking at young men have sex on his phone. He didn't care about what people thought, and that's what I liked about Phil. He didn't care about people and their thoughts. He was, as Matthew McConaughey would say, "L-I-V-I-N Man."

The next story is one that was truly a sad day at the facility. The next story is about one of my favorite patients who sadly passed away.

This resident was one of my favorite residents. She was admitted to the facility for rehab services and was receiving care; however, because of her insurance, she was constantly being told that she only was given two more days—that is, two more days for services. This individual was clearly in need for more time at the facility, but her insurance said no. Sidebar, don't get terrible insurance or cheap insurance. It may seem nice on the surface, but in the long run, it's terrible. The insurance agencies like to dictate how long you are able to go to a rehab facility and what care you can get. Essentially, they want you to have the shortest time available and then get you out. That's what happened to this lovely lady.

One day, after being told again that her insurance was getting cancelled, she got clearly upset. She was crying and upset at the situation at hand. I comforted her in the best way possible and, per her request, let her have some time alone. A few hours later, I saw several people run past my office in a panic. I step out to see what the commotion was; and I found out that the individual whom I saw a few hours ago, my favorite person, had suddenly stopped breathing. And thus a code-blue call was issued.

As a nonmedical individual, there was not much that I could do to help this situation. The only thing that I could do was help direct the ambulance drivers to her room and help with crowd control as there was a group gathering. In working with crowd control, one of my duties was to ensure that all of the doors in the residents' hallways were closed. I made sure that all of the doors were closed and helped out where I could. As I closed the final door, I saw down the hall the paramedics pushing the gurney with the resident on it down the hall to their ambulance. They went past me with such speed I felt like they were going 20mph. The next thing that I saw will be something that I'll never get out of my head.

I saw my favorite resident lying on the gurney, topless, her face with shades of purple and blue, and her eyes bloodshot. The paramedics rushed her to their ambulance and worked on her as much as they could, but after several minutes of working to revive her, she was gone. We could tell that she was gone when they brought her in the hallway to the ambulance. That look is a look that you just cannot unsee.

The resident's husband came to the facility shortly after the ambulance took his wife to the hospital. He had no idea what was going on. He entered the facility and went to her room and inquired where she was. I had to be the one to tell him of the news of his wife having a code blue and what we had done. I was the one who had to tell him about her trip to the hospital. I was the one who was being screamed at because of his anger and frustration of how things were handled. I was the one on the frontline of their emotions.

That's what happens in nursing homes. You are the one on the frontlines dealing with emotions, be them happy or angry or sad. You are the one who are seen as heroes or bad guys. You are the one who get hugs and happy stories or get to witness instances that you would never think you would ever see. Again, I'm not trying to scare you or shock you about what you may see or may not see because everyone's experience is different. This is just an insight to something that I have seen as my time as a social worker working in a nursing home. If you do decide to do this route, good for you. People need people like you. Find your purpose, find your favorite resident, find your Phil.

PART 6

Hospice

CHAPTER 20

I wish I can say that my time at the nursing home was going to be the end all and be all of my social-work career, but that's not true. I had a terrible boss at the facility who did not care about the residents, their concerns, or their safety. This was one issue that I had with working at a nursing home: the administrators. Many of them are great, but sometimes you get a bad egg, and it ruins things for you. That's what happened to me, and I found myself back into the job pool and landed a job in hospice care.

Hospice was something that I always thought about doing but wasn't sure if it was right for me. I felt like talking with people who were dying was going to be boring and "what could you do as a social worker in hospice?" Turns out, a lot. You are there for the patient and their families. You are there to help provide support for their loved ones and be there as a companion for the client. Hospice is such a hard work to say and handle because many people think that once they enter this service, that's it. They are dead. That's not true. Hospice is much more than that. Many people who enter hospice services sometimes graduate off the services, and some stay on for long periods of time.

Hospice shouldn't be a negative word, nor should it be a scary word to say. Hospice can be scary, sure, but is also can be comforting and helpful for the client and their loved ones too. I wish I could say that I had a great story about working at hospice, but unfortunately, I don't. I only stayed about three months before I switched into my present setting, schools. I do however have instances of working with hospice on a personal level and professional level.

In my time as a hospital social worker, I was set on the oncology unit and thus had to refer a lot of clients to hospice. In the area that I had worked, there were a lot of hospice agencies, as I'm sure there is all over the world, but one agency that was local to me was one of the best. Because of confidentiality, I won't be naming the facility, but I will say that it is one of the better ones in the area that I reside. I have worked with them several times for my clients, and then when it came time for a loved one of mine to enter hospice, this agency was a no-brainer. This agency was fantastic, from the time they had received the referral to the time they had the equipment and my loved one home was incredible.

The loved one who had entered hospice was only on their services for a short time, but I knew that they were there for not only them but also my family. Once my loved one passed away, a representative from the hospice agency had come to the funeral to pay their respects and to be there for us. They not only did that, but they also provided grief services for up to a year for our family, free of charge.

In my mind, I had a feeling that hospice could be a fun and interesting career, but with so many options out there, I was unsure of which one I wanted to use. It was not until after the funeral of my loved one and was able to see the compassion that they had provided that I knew this was the one for me. So once I was fed up with my nursing home boss and her unethical and illegal practices (don't worry, she's been reported to the state several times), I found myself with new employment at this hospice agency.

I enjoyed this field for the most part, but a lot of it was just companionship and talking to individuals who were dying. As much as I didn't mind this, a lot of the clients did not want to talk. They did not want to speak with a new stranger about their life. They just wanted to relax and sleep. They didn't want to be bothered, which I totally understand. I wouldn't either, but I felt like I wanted more out of life. I wanted to help people, and I wanted to help educate people, so when an opportunity came to work in a school, I jumped on it.

PART 7

Schools

CHAPTER

21

I had received a call from an elementary school to be a school social worker for an elementary school in a town about forty-five minutes from me. I felt that this was perfect for me. I get to work in a school, I get summer break and winter break off, I get to work and interact with little kids—this was perfect! I accepted the position about a week into the school year; and with me being an outsider to not only the community, but also the school organization that I worked for, I knew that I had a lot to show. I knew that I had to make a presence for myself.

I entered the school and was given a classroom as my "office." I was so excited to have my own classroom in which I could decorate it and do with it as I wanted to. I spent the first week at the elementary school decorating the office, going around, and meeting the different staff as well as the students. It was awesome! I felt like I could get used to this—until I didn't.

I thought that this career path was going to be great, but you see, I didn't have any training. I didn't have a social worker to follow. I didn't have a handbook to follow. I wasn't told what to do and what not to do. I literally was thrown in a classroom and essentially was told "figure it out." I felt discouraged because I wanted to do the best that I could, but how could I when there was no support or someone to show me what to do. I felt like I was thrown into a giant ocean with no knowledge of how to swim and was told, "Well, swim or die. Choice is yours."

CHAPTER

22

One day after trying to figure out what the hell I was supposed to do, I had received a phone call from my now employer asking me if I wanted to come work for them as a high-school counselor. I answered the phone and told them, “No, thank you. I actually have a job right now, but I thank you for the offer.” I then hung up and thought about what I had just said. Did I really just tell them no? A job opportunity that was much closer to home, in my community, and with people that I *actually* knew? What the hell was I thinking? Of course, I made a mistake. I called them back and apologized for the quick no and stated that I would love to come in for an interview. We set this up for a few days away, and then I waited.

The day of the interview, I was nervous. I mean, who else isn’t nervous on a job interview? It’s scary! I arrived at the high school where I had graduated from, and it felt like home, even though high school was just that for me, high school. I came and did my schooling, got my diploma, and left. Nothing fancy.

I entered the conference room and met with the principal as well as associate principal, both of which were there when I was in high school. It felt like a blast from the past. I interviewed and they asked me when I could start. I asked them when they would like to have me and they stated, “Uhm, last week.” We laughed, and we came to a conclusion of two weeks from that day. I left feeling great that I will be starting a new career path yet scared as I knew nothing of working in a high school, let alone as a high-school counselor.

I just want to take a minute to say how much I love my job too. I get to work with older kids, still get to have a nice schedule, and I feel so much better with my mental health. Sometimes it takes several instances to find your niche, and well, I've found mine.

PART 8

Don't Ever Give Up! You Got This!

CHAPTER

23

You're probably, "Wait a minute, I thought this was a book about true stories from a social worker and certain things that we could experience." You'd be right. This book is a book about true stories from a social worker and certain experiences that you may see, but I also wanted to let you know that you don't have to just stay in the social-work field. You can branch out to other areas as well, such as school counseling.

The world of social work is amazing. You can experience so many things in this profession, be it hospital, child services, nursing homes, or hospice care. Whatever you do, just know, you have options for any career path. I also want to say that whatever you do, don't ever give up! You got this! There may be times when you think that you chose the wrong career path or you don't know if you can handle it. Just know, you can. You're a badass, and you can achieve greatness. Don't ever give up on your dreams and aspirations. So what if it may take several jobs or years to find what you like or what you want to do, and so what if it's not in the social-work field? That's okay! You must take care of you and your mental health.

I hope this book has been somewhat insightful into what it is a social worker can do and what a social worker has seen in their time.

Keep fighting the good fight!

www.ingramcontent.com/pod-product-compliance
Lightning Source LLC
Chambersburg PA
CBHW032208040426
42449CB00005B/500
979889285l565